ODYSSEUS
ESCAPING POSEIDON'S CURSE

A
GREEK
LEGEND

GRAPHIC
UNIVERSE™

STORY BY
DAN JOLLEY

PENCILS AND INKS BY
THOMAS YEATES

EUROPE

ITALY

SARDINIA

4

8

BALEARIC
ISLANDS

5

3

NORTH

THE FOLLOWING SITES AND MYTHICAL
ENCOUNTERS ARE LOCATED ON THIS MAP,
WHICH SHOWS SOME MODERN BORDERS
AND PLACE NAMES.

1 TROY

2 THE LOTUS EATERS

3 CYCLOPES

4 CIRCE

5 SIRENS

6 SCYLLA AND CHARYBDIS

7 HELIOS

8 CALYPSO

9 ITHACA

2

ODYSSEUS
ESCAPING POSEIDON'S CURSE

A GREEK LEGEND

GREECE

1

TURKEY

6

SICILY

7

9

MEDITERRANEAN SEA

AFRICA

GRAPHIC UNIVERSE™ • MINNEAPOLIS

This book is based on the *Odyssey*, an epic poem believed to have been written around 700 B.C. Tradition has it that the story was written by Homer, a blind Greek poet. But historians cannot confirm this, and even Homer's existence has been questioned. Regardless, the epic story of Odysseus' journey home after the Trojan War (c. 1200 B.C.) is one of the greatest works in all of world literature.

Author Dan Jolley adapted the story to fit the Graphic Myths and Legends forty-page format, referencing several translations of the Greek classic. Artist Thomas Yeates used historical and traditional sources for visual details—from images on ancient Greek vases to sculpture and other artwork. Professor David Mulroy of the University of Wisconsin-Milwaukee ensured historical and visual accuracy.

STORY BY DAN JOLLEY

PENCILS AND INKS BY THOMAS YEATES
WITH SAM GLANZMAN AND KEN HOOPER

COLORING AND LETTERING BY
HI-FI COLOUR DESIGN

CONSULTANT: DAVID MULROY, PH.D.,
UNIVERSITY OF WISCONSIN—MILWAUKEE

Graphic Universe™
A division of Lerner Publishing Group, Inc.
241 First Avenue North
Minneapolis, MN 55401 USA

For reading levels and more information, look up this title at www.lernerbooks.com.

Library of Congress Cataloging-in-Publication Data

Jolley, Dan.
    Odysseus : escaping Poseidon's curse : a Greek legend / story by Dan Jolley ; pencils and inks by Thomas Yeates.
        p.   cm. — (Graphic myths and legends)
    Includes index.
    ISBN-13: 978-0-8225-6208-5 (lib. bdg. : alk. paper)
    ISBN-13: 978-1-58013-631-0 (eb pdf)
    1. Odysseus (Greek mythology)—Juvenile literature. 2. Poseidon (Greek deity)—Juvenile literature. I. Yeates, Thomas. II. Title.
    BL820.O3J65   2008
    741.5'973—dc22   2007001827

Manufactured in the United States of America
6 - 43018 - 5251 - 2/7/2018

TABLE OF CONTENTS

THE JOURNEY BEGINS

The TROJAN WAR. AN EPIC STRUGGLE, SPANNING YEARS.

COUNTLESS BATTLES, FILLED WITH STAGGERING DEATH AND DESTRUCTION ALL FOUGHT FOR THE BEAUTY OF ONE WOMAN.

THE LEGENDARY *HELEN OF TROY*

IT WAS A WAR WAGED BY *HEROES* ... FIERCE WARRIORS, BRILLIANT STRATEGISTS. THEIR NAMES, TOO, HAVE BECOME LEGEND.

HECTOR. ACHILLES. PARIS. AND THE MOST CUNNING FIGHTER OF ALL ...

ODYSSEUS, KING OF ITHACA. FAVORED BY ATHENA, GODDESS OF WISDOM.

IT WAS HE WHO ENGINEERED THE TROJAN HORSE, A HUGE WOODEN STATUE THAT HID A GROUP OF GREEK WARRIORS INSIDE.

THE TROJANS WERE FOOLED INTO BRINGING THE HORSE INTO THEIR CITY. THAT TRICKERY LED TO THE FALL OF TROY.

ODYSSEUS NEVER WANTED TO FIGHT IN THE WAR. HE WANTED ONLY TO REMAIN IN ITHACA.

TEND HIS LANDS. STAY WITH HIS FAMILY – HIS BELOVED WIFE, PENELOPE, AND HIS SON, TELEMACHUS.

AND NOW, NOW THAT THE LONG, PUNISHING WAR WAS FINALLY OVER ...

ODYSSEUS MEANT TO RETURN TO HIS HOME, LETTING NOTHING AND NO ONE STAND IN HIS WAY.

A SQUADRON OF SHIPS FILLED WITH FINE GREEK WARRIORS ACCOMPANIED HIM AS HE SET SAIL FROM TROY, HOMEWARD BOUND.

BUT ODYSSEUS WAS UNAWARE THAT HIS ACTIONS IN THE WAR HAD ANGERED SOME OF THE GODS ...

... NAMELY *ZEUS*, LORD OF LIGHTNING, AND SEA-DWELLING *POSEIDON*, GOD OF EARTHQUAKES. ATHENA'S FAVOR COULD NOT PROTECT ODYSSEUS FROM THEM.

SHORTLY AFTER THE SHIPS LEFT TROY, THE DISPLEASURE OF THE GODS MADE ITSELF FELT ...

... WITH SAVAGE FURY.

ROW, MEN, ROW FOR YOUR *LIVES!*

ROW UNTIL YOUR MUSCLES *RIP* AND YOUR *BONES CRACK!*

THERE!

WE CAN MAKE *LANDFALL!*

NOW *ROW!*

IN THEIR DESPERATION TO ESCAPE THE STORM'S WRATH, ODYSSEUS AND HIS CREW HAD ARRIVED IN THE LAND OF THE *LOTUS EATERS*.

NOT MUCH WAS KNOWN OF THE INHABITANTS OF THIS LAND ...

... THOUGH ODYSSEUS WOULD SOON LEARN MORE ABOUT THEM THAN HE EVER WANTED TO KNOW.

WITH HIS MOST TRUSTED CAPTAIN, *EURYLOCHUS*, ODYSSEUS SPOKE TO TWO SCOUTS AND A RUNNER ...

...SENDING THEM TO EXPLORE THIS UNFAMILIAR LAND AND REPORT THEIR FINDINGS TO HIM.

THE SUN WAS HIGH IN THE SKY WHEN THE MEN LEFT.

BUT LONG AFTER NIGHTFALL, THEY STILL HAD NOT RETURNED.

THE NEXT DAY, ODYSSEUS LEFT *EURYLOCHUS* IN COMMAND AND HEADED INLAND, SEARCHING FOR HIS MISSING MEN.

ODYSSEUS WASTED NO TIME IN **DRIVING** THE THREE MEN BACK TO THE SHIPS.

THAT WAS THE **ONLY** WAY HE COULD OVERCOME THE POWER OF THE LOTUS.

FOR, AS HE DISCOVERED, ONCE A MAN ATE OF THE LOTUS FLOWER, ALL RATIONAL THOUGHT FLED HIS MIND. ALL OF HIS DESIRE FOCUSED ON THE PLANT ITSELF.

BREAK CAMP!

WE ARE **LEAVING!**

SO STRONG WAS THE POWER OF THE PLANT THAT THE THREE SAILORS HAD TO BE **TIED DOWN** ...

... OTHERWISE THEY WOULD HAVE DESERTED, AND RETURNED TO THE LOTUS EATERS' VILLAGE.

DISGUSTED AND DETERMINED NOT TO LOSE ANY OF HIS CREW TO SO **SENSELESS** A THREAT, ODYSSEUS SET SAIL AT **ONCE.**

THE FURY OF THE CYCLOPS

*But several nights later, his progress was **slowed** by a fog thicker than any he'd ever seen.*

CAPTAIN! ODYSSEUS! WE CANNOT SEE A *THING*, SIR!

PERHAPS WE SHOULD DROP ANCHOR AND REMAIN HERE!

NO EURYLOCHUS.

WE ARE NEAR LAND. I CAN *FEEL* IT.

BUT *HOW*, CAPTAIN?

HOW COULD YOU KNOW SUCH A TH—

WHRRNNCH

WHAT WAS THAT YOU WERE ASKING ME, EURYLOCHUS?

I'LL ... BE SETTING UP CAMP WITH THE REST OF THE MEN.

UPON ARRIVAL, THEY FOUND THEMSELVES *DEEPLY* IMPRESSED ... NOT JUST WITH HOW WELL STOCKED THE CAVE WAS, BUT WITH ITS SHEER SIZE.

ODYSSEUS, LET US *TAKE* ALL OF THIS!

TAKE IT, RUN BACK DOWN TO THE SHIP AND BE ON OUR WAY!

NO.

I WANT TO *MEET* THIS CAVEMAN.

FIND OUT WHAT SORT OF PERSON HE IS.

BY THE BLACKENED SKIN OF *HEPHAISTOS* ...

BUT WHEN THE CAVE'S OWNER RETURNED, ODYSSEUS QUICKLY REALIZED HIS ERROR IN JUDGMENT...

...AS HE AND HIS CREW TOOK *REFUGE* IN THE BACK OF THE CAVERN.

POLYPHEMUS THE CYCLOPS WAS *HUGE* AND THE POWER IN HIS LIMBS *OBVIOUS*. ODYSSEUS' HEART SANK IN HIS CHEST ...

... AS HE WATCHED THE CREATURE BLOCK THE CAVERN'S ENTRANCE WITH A STONE SO HEAVY IT WOULD HAVE TAKEN TWO DOZEN TEAMS OF HORSES TO MOVE IT.

BUT IF ODYSSEUS' HEART SANK AT THE SIGHT OF THE BRUTE'S *STRENGTH*, HIS *BLOOD STOPPED* IN HIS VEINS AS THE CYCLOPS SPOTTED HIM.

WHO ARE YOU?

WHY HAVE YOU COME HERE?

WE ARE ACHAEANS, GOOD SIR, FRESH FROM THE WAR IN TROY.

BLOWN OFF COURSE ON OUR JOURNEY HOME.

OFF COURSE, IS IT? WHERE HAVE YOU LEFT IT?

OUR SHIP ... WAS BROKEN UP UPON THE ROCKS.

WE ARE *SURVIVORS*, THESE MEN AND I.

WE ASK ONLY FOR WHAT HELP OR GIFTS YOU MIGHT GIVE US ... AND PRAY THAT YOU HONOR ZEUS AND AID US, AS IS CUSTOM.

AND FINALLY, BY MORNING, HE HAD THE SOLUTION.

THERE YOU GO, MY LITTLE ONES.

OUT TO YOUR PASTURE.

THANKS TO HIS CUNNING, ODYSSEUS LED THE ESCAPE FROM THE CYCLOPS' CLUTCHES ...

... AND WOULD HAVE GOTTEN AWAY SCOT-FREE.

BUT HE HAD TO RUB IT IN.

CYCLOPS! IF ANYONE ASKS WHO BEAT AND BLINDED YOU, TELL THEM IT WAS ODYSSEUS!

RAIDER OF CITIES, SON OF LAERTES!

ODYSSEUS, KING OF ITHACA!

THE CYCLOPS POLYPHEMUS *RAGED* AT THIS TAUNTING. HE HURLED HUGE BOULDERS OUT TO SEA, TRYING TO CRUSH ODYSSEUS AND HIS SHIP.

BUT WHEN THAT FAILED, HE TOOK A DIFFERENT TACTIC — AND PRAYED TO HIS *FATHER*, THE SEA-GOD *POSEIDON*, TO PUT A CURSE ON THE NAME HE NOW KNEW.

AND THE DOOM THAT POSEIDON CALLED DOWN UPON ODYSSEUS WOULD HAUNT HIM FOR *YEARS* TO COME.

THE MAGIC OF THE
ISLAND WITCH

SOON ENOUGH, TRAGEDY BEFELL ODYSSEUS.

HE AND HIS MEN STOPPED TO TAKE ON WATER, AND ENCOUNTERED THE *LAISTRYGONIANS*.

... A RACE OF *GIANTS* JUST AS SAVAGE AS POLYPHEMUS THE CYCLOPS.

ODYSSEUS AND HIS SHIP ESCAPED THEIR HARBOR BY THE THINNEST OF MARGINS.

BUT THE OTHER ELEVEN SHIPS, CREWS AND ALL, WERE *DESTROYED*.

WITH A HEART HEAVY WITH SADNESS AND REGRET, ODYSSEUS AND HIS REMAINING MEN MADE LANDFALL ...

... ON *AIAIA*, AN ISLAND UNKNOWN TO THEM.

ODYSSEUS DIVIDED HIS MEN INTO TWO GROUPS, ONE UNDER HIS WATCH, THE OTHER LED BY EURYLOCHUS ...

BARELY ABLE TO BREATHE, EURYLOCHUS TOLD ODYSSEUS EVERYTHING HE HAD SEEN.

AND GRIM THOUGH THE SITUATION WAS, ODYSSEUS SAW NO OTHER CHOICE BUT TO GO HIMSELF AND TRY TO RESCUE HIS MEN.

BUT ON HIS WAY TO CIRCE'S HOUSE, HE RECEIVED A VISIT FROM A *MOST* UNEXPECTED SOURCE.

HERMES!

MESSENGER OF THE *GODS* ... HOW MAY I *SERVE* YOU?

RISE, ODYSSEUS. YOUR MEN HAVE FALLEN PREY TO CIRCE'S VILE SORCERY.

BUT YOU CAN YET ESCAPE, FOR MY SISTER *ATHENA* STILL FAVORS YOU.

TAKE THIS. IT IS THE PLANT MOLY, AND IT WILL SHIELD YOU FROM THE WITCH'S CHARMS.

BAFFLED BUT VERY GRATEFUL, ODYSSEUS FASTENED THE SPRIG TO HIS CLOTHING LIKE A TALISMAN AND CONTINUED ON HIS WAY.

SOON ...

GREETINGS WEARY TRAVELER! WELCOME TO MY HOME. I AM CIRCE.

WON'T YOU COME INSIDE, AND LET ME OFFER YOU FOOD AND DRINK?

I APPRECIATE YOUR HOSPITALITY, MY LADY, AND ACCEPT.

PERHAPS YOU CAN HELP ME FURTHER, AS WELL. I SEEK A NUMBER OF MY CREW, WHO SEEM TO HAVE GOTTEN LOST.

PERHAPS. PERHAPS I CAN HELP YOU AT THAT.

WHAT OF THE MEAL, TRAVELER? DO YOU FIND IT PLEASING?

PLEASING ENOUGH, YES, MY LADY. BUT I MUST ASK YOU AGAIN WHAT YOU KNOW OF MY MEN ...

YOUR MEN? YOUR MEN ARE SWINE, AS YOU SHALL NOW BE!

SWINE, IS IT? SO THOSE CREATURES OUTSIDE REALLY ARE MY CREW!

YOU SHALL NOT WORK YOUR SORCERY ON ME, WITCH! NOT ON ODYSSEUS OF ITHACA!

25

AND SO ODYSSEUS AND HIS CREW ACCEPTED CIRCE'S OFFER.

THE MEN MADE CIRCE'S HOME THEIR OWN.

BUT MONTH FOLLOWED MONTH, SEASON FOLLOWED SEASON, AND THE MEN FINALLY REALIZED THEY HAD STAYED ON CIRCE'S ISLAND FOR A *YEAR*.

EURYLOCHUS AND A FEW OTHERS APPROACHED ODYSSEUS, BEGGING HIM TO SHAKE OFF THE *TRANCE* THAT KEPT HIM THERE.

THE ISLAND OF AIAIA WAS BEAUTIFUL, AND FOR A TIME SEEMED LIKE A *PARADISE*, FREE OF THE DANGERS THAT HAD PLAGUED THEM FOR SO LONG.

... AND TO SET SAIL ONCE AGAIN FOR HIS DISTANT HOME OF ITHACA.

27

ODYSSEUS HEARD HIS MEN'S PLEAS. HE BROKE FROM HIS PLEASANT STUPOR, AND MADE CIRCE AWARE OF HIS INTENTION TO TAKE HIS MEN AND LEAVE.

THIS CAUSED HER GREAT ANGUISH, FOR SHE HAD GROWN VERY CLOSE TO ODYSSEUS.

BUT SHE WAS GRACIOUS ENOUGH TO *WARN* HIM OF THE DANGERS THAT LAY AHEAD OF HIM ON HIS PATH.

THE FIRST DANGER WAS THE *SIRENS* – MYSTERIOUS, DEADLY WOMEN WHOSE SONGS PULLED MEN UNCONTROLLABLY TO THEM.

NEXT WAS *SCYLLA* – A TWELVE-LEGGED, SIX-HEADED MONSTROSITY THAT DEVOURED SIX MEN OUT OF EVERY CREW THAT PASSED HER.

"DO NOT ATTEMPT TO FIGHT HER," CIRCE WARNED, "FOR SHE IS AN EVIL THAT CANNOT BE KILLED."

LASTY, VERY NEAR SCYLLA LAY *CHARYBDIS*, A GIANT *WHIRLPOOL* THAT SPELLED UTTER DISASTER FOR ANY SHIP CAUGHT IN IT.

ARMED WITH THIS KNOWLEDGE, ODYSSEUS SAID GOOD-BYE TO CIRCE.

HE DID NOT LOOK BACK... AND SO DID NOT SEE THE *TEARS* SHE SHED AT HIS DEPARTURE.

AN ORDEAL OF MONSTERS

SHORTLY AFTER LEAVING CIRCE, ODYSSEUS ENCOUNTERED THE FIRST SIGN SHE HAD TOLD HIM TO WATCH FOR.

A *DEAD CALM* ON THE WATER. ODYSSEUS KNEW THIS HERALDED THE LAND OF THE *SIRENS*, BUT THANKS TO CIRCE HE WAS PREPARED.

WARMING BITS OF BEESWAX IN HIS HANDS, HE FASHIONED *PLUGS...*

...AND SEALED UP HIS CREW'S *EARS*, SO THAT THE SIRENS' SONG COULDN'T REACH THEM.

BUT ODYSSEUS HIMSELF WAS *CURIOUS...* AND HE ASKED EURYLOCHUS TO LASH HIM TO THE MAST, HIS EARS UNCOVERED.

"DO NOT UNTIE ME UNDER ANY CIRCUMSTANCES," ODYSSEUS TOLD THEM. "AND IF I PROTEST, ONLY TIE ME TIGHTER AND WITH MORE ROPE."

STEADILY ONWARD THE SHIP MOVED, THE CREW'S EARS PLUGGED AND THE CAPTAIN BOUND TO THE MAST.

AND SOON ENOUGH...

...A BEAUTIFUL, *EERIE SONG* FLOATED ACROSS THE WATER TO ODYSSEUS.

A SONG SO POWERFUL, SO OVERWHELMING, IT WAS AS IF ANGELS THEMSELVES WERE SINGING.

AND EVEN THOUGH ODYSSEUS KNEW THE SIRENS WOULD TEMPT ANY MAN WHO CAME NEAR THEM, CAUSING THEM TO LINGER AND LISTEN UNTIL THEY WASTE AWAY TO NOTHING ...

CUT ME LOOSE! RIGHT *NOW*, YOU DOGS, THAT'S AN *ORDER*!

...THE EFFECT SOON *OVERPOWERED* HIM.

UNTIE ME!

UNTIE ME NOW!

... AND ONLY TIED ODYSSEUS MORE TIGHTLY, SCREAM AND WRITHE THOUGH HE DID.

ODYSSEUS WOULD HAVE KILLED EVERY MAN ON THE SHIP TO REACH THE SIRENS, BUT THE ROPES HELD TIGHT.

AND SOON THE SIREN SONG FADED AWAY ON THE MIST, RELEASING HIM.

A FEW DAYS PASSED, AND – EXACTLY AS CIRCE HAD SAID IT WOULD – THE SEA BEGAN TO GROW ROUGH AND CHOPPY ...

...JUST AS THE SHIP APPROACHED A NARROW **STRAIT.**

THIS WAS THE HOME OF BOTH **SCYLLA** AND **CHARYBDIS** ... ONE ON THE LEFT WALL, THE OTHER ON THE RIGHT.

"DO NOT APPROACH CHARYBDIS," CIRCE HAD TOLD ODYSSEUS, "FOR THAT WOULD MEAN CERTAIN DEATH."

"SCYLLA WILL TAKE SIX OF YOUR MEN. THERE IS NOTHING YOU CAN DO TO PREVENT THAT. SIMPLY ROW AS FAST AS YOU CAN, SO AS NOT TO LOSE **TWELVE."**

ODYSSEUS LOOKED UP AND SAW THE ENTRANCE TO SCYLLA'S DEN, WHICH LOOKED JUST AS CIRCE HAD DESCRIBED.

HE HADN'T TOLD HIS MEN ABOUT THE MONSTER. IF HER ATTACK WAS UNAVOIDABLE, THERE WAS NO NEED TO CAUSE THEM WORRY.

AND YET, IN HIS HEART, ODYSSEUS WANTED TO *FIGHT* SCYLLA, AND GLADLY WOULD HAVE ...

... IF NOT FOR *CHARYBDIS.* THE VORTEX DRANK THE OCEAN DOWN, THEN SPEWED IT BACK UP WITH IMMENSE FORCE, OVER AND OVER AGAIN.

AND WHEN ONE SUCH WAVE SLAMMED INTO THE SHIP, DEMANDING THE FULL ATTENTION OF ALL ON BOARD ...

SCYLLA *STRUCK*, LIGHTNING FAST, AND TOOK SIX MEN WITHOUT A SOUND.

TERROR LENT NEW STRENGTH TO THE CREW'S MUSCLES, AND THEY ROWED FASTER THAN EVER BEFORE ...

... TAKING THEM SWIFTLY OUT OF DANGER'S REACH.

BUT NO SOONER HAD THEY ESCAPED THE THREAT OF *DEATH* ... THAN *TEMPTATION* REARED ITS UGLY HEAD.

LOOK AT THAT *HERD!* LET US HAVE SOME *BEEF,* BROTHERS!

NO. YOU MAY NOT.

WHAT? *WHY* NOT, CAPTAIN?

THIS IS THE CATTLE OF *HELIOS,* CIRCE'S FATHER AND GOD OF THE NOONDAY SUN! HE PRIZES IT GREATLY!

DOOM WILL FALL ON THE HEADS OF ANY MEN WHO HARM IT. CIRCE HAS TOLD ME THIS AND I BELIEVE IT TO BE TRUE.

THAT HERD OF CATTLE WILL GO *UNTOUCHED.*

A TEMPTATION TOO GREAT

THE CREW DID NOT CARE FOR THIS DECISION AT ALL, AND THEY PLEADED AND ARGUED WITH ODYSSEUS.

"AT LEAST LET US GO ASHORE AND TAKE ON WATER," THEY ASKED. "WE WON'T TOUCH THE CATTLE. WE JUST WANT TO FEEL DRY LAND UNDER OUR FEET."

ODYSSEUS AGREED ...

... BUT THE MEN HAD NOT TASTED FRESH BEEF IN SOME TIME, AND TENSION STILL RAN HIGH AMONG THE CREW.

THIS TENSION WAS MADE MUCH WORSE WHEN *FOUL WEATHER* PREVENTED THEM FROM LEAVING – FOR A SOLID *MONTH.*

RATIONS RAN LOW, THE MEN GREW HUNGRY... AND STILL THE FAT, HEALTHY CATTLE GRAZED NEARBY.

FINALLY THE TEMPTATION GREW TOO MUCH. WHILE ODYSSEUS HAD LEFT THE CAMP TO MEDITATE AND PRAY ...

... EURYLOCHUS AND THE REST OF THE CREW *KILLED* SEVERAL OF THE COWS AND BEGAN TO COOK THEM OVER OPEN FIRES.

ODYSSEUS SMELLED THIS TREACHERY LONG BEFORE HE LAID EYES ON IT.

THE CREW HAD BETRAYED HIM, AND THEREFORE BETRAYED *HELIOS.* ODYSSEUS KNEW FULL WELL THEY WERE *DOOMED.*

35

THERE WAS NOTHING HE COULD DO ABOUT IT, THOUGH, AND A SHORT WHILE LATER THE FOUL WEATHER FINALLY TURNED.

THE CREW HURRIEDLY BROKE CAMP AND SET SAIL, DETERMINED TO TAKE ADVANTAGE OF IT.

GREAT HELIOS ... AGAIN, I BEG *FORGIVENESS.*

BUT HELIOS HAD SEEN HOW ODYSSEUS' MEN HAD TREATED HIS CATTLE, AND APPEALED TO *ZEUS,* KING OF THE GODS, LORD OF STORMS.

ZEUS WILLINGLY *OBLIGED.*

KRAK·KRAK·KOOOM

SO, THEN, THE DOOM PLAYED OUT, AS THE FURY OF THE GODS LEFT ONLY ONE SURVIVOR – ODYSSEUS HIMSELF.

FOR A FEW MOMENTS, ODYSSEUS BELIEVED THAT HIS FATE COULD NOT BE ANY WORSE ...

... BUT THEN HE SAW WHERE THE HOWLING WINDS AND SLAMMING CURRENTS OF THE STORM HAD TAKEN HIM ...

... STRAIGHT BACK TO *CHARYBDIS.*

WITH THE LAST FEW OUNCES OF STRENGTH LEFT IN HIM, ODYSSEUS *JUMPED* ...

... AND WATCHED AS THE FINAL BIT OF WRECKAGE FROM HIS ONCE-PROUD SHIP WAS TAKEN DOWN TO THE OCEAN'S FLOOR.

FOR WHAT FELT LIKE HOURS, ODYSSEUS HUNG THERE, TRAPPED – UNTIL THE WHIRLPOOL *SPEWED* OUT THE BIT OF WOOD HE HAD CLUNG TO FOR SO LONG.

LEAPING DOWN INTO THE SPRAY, ODYSSEUS REGAINED HIS WRECKAGE AND MADE HIS WAY BACK OUT TO SEA AS FAST AS HE WAS ABLE.

HOW LONG DID ODYSSEUS DRIFT, THEN, ALONE ON THE OCEAN? HOURS? DAYS? HE DIDN'T KNOW.

HE ONLY KNEW THAT WHEN HE REGAINED CONCIOUSNESS ...

... AND OPENED HIS EYES ...

CALYPSO'S EMBRACE

... HE WAS GREETED WITH SUCH BEAUTY THAT AT FIRST HE BELIEVED HE HAD DIED AND GONE TO PARADISE.

WELCOME, WANDERER.

MY NAME IS CALYPSO.

EVEN MORE BEAUTIFUL THAN CIRCE WAS CALYPSO, A MAGICAL NYMPH OF THE SEA.

CALYPSO IMMEDIATELY FELL IN LOVE WITH ODYSSEUS. SHE FED HIM, CLOTHED HIM...

... AND LET IT BE KNOWN THAT IF HE STAYED THERE, WITH HER, HE WOULD NEVER AGE, NEVER KNOW ANY PHYSICAL WANT OR NEED.

BUT ANOTHER TRUTH SOON REVEALED ITSELF: CALYPSO WAS NOT ASKING. ODYSSEUS WAS MAGICALLY FORCED TO REMAIN THERE WITH HER.

HELPLESS IN THE FACE OF ENCHANTMENT, ODYSSEUS STAYED THERE ON CALYPSO'S ISLAND AS THE SEASONS CHANGED AND CHANGED AGAIN ...

... AND THE *YEARS* FLED PAST, ONE AFTER ANOTHER. ODYSSEUS GREW SAD AND HOMESICK, HIS BROKEN HEART LONGING FOR HIS WIFE AND SON.

BUT THOUGH SHE KNEW OF ODYSSEUS' ANGUISH, STILL CALYPSO WANTED HIM.

AND SO THERE HE STAYED, UNDER HER CONTROL.

FINALLY, ONE DAY, THE HALLS OF *MOUNT OLYMPUS*, HOME OF THE GODS, RANG WITH ANGRY FOOTFALLS.

... BECAUSE ATHENA, GODDESS OF WISDOM, HAD FINALLY HAD ENOUGH.

LORD ZEUS! MAY I SPEAK WITH YOU?

ATHENA HAD LONG FELT SORRY FOR ODYSSEUS. NOW SHE PLEADED WITH THE RULER OF THE GODS.

PLEASE, LORD ZEUS.

HE HAS SUFFERED ENOUGH.

ATHENA. WHAT CONCERNS YOU?

SEND WORD TO CALYPSO THE SEA NYMPH THAT HE SHOULD BE LET *GO*.

LET ODYSSEUS REJOIN HIS *FAMILY*.

ATHENA'S WORDS HAD THE EFFECT SHE HOPED FOR: ZEUS SENT HERMES TO CALYPSO'S ISLAND ...

... WITH NEWS THAT THE SEA NYMPH WOULD **NOT** WANT TO HEAR.

HERMES! I HAVEN'T SEEN YOU IN SUCH A LONG TIME!

PLEASE, COME IN, LET ME BRING YOU SOME WINE!

I CANNOT STAY, CALYPSO. I MERELY BRING WORD TO YOU FROM LORD ZEUS:

SEND HIM HOME.

IT IS ZEUS' WILL THAT YOU SHOULD RELEASE THE MORTAL HERO ODYSSEUS.

CALYPSO TOOK THE NEWS BITTERLY. "I CANNOT SEND HIM!" SHE TOLD HERMES. "I HAVE NO BOATS OR OARSMEN!"

HE HAS STAYED HERE, AWAY FROM HIS LIFE, LONG ENOUGH.

BUT FINALLY SHE DID DECIDE TO LET HIM LEAVE, MUCH AS SHE HATED TO.

YES?

I ... HAVE DECIDED TO LET YOU GO. BUILD A **RAFT** ... TAKE IT OUT TO SEA.

RETURN TO YOUR WIFE AND SON.

AFTER **ALL** THESE YEARS, YOU SING THIS TUNE NOW?

I'LL TAKE NO **RAFT** ANYWHERE ... UNLESS YOU MAKE ME AN **OATH**.

ODYSSEUS ... I MUST SPEAK WITH YOU.

AN OATH? WHAT SHALL I PROMISE?

SWEAR TO ME THAT YOU'LL WORK NO MORE **ENCHANTMENT** THAT WILL CAUSE ME **HARM**.

MY DEAR SWEET MAN. I MAKE YOU THAT PROMISE **GLADLY.**

COME. I CANNOT SEND YOU AWAY ON ANY GREAT SHIP ...

...BUT I CAN ALLOW YOU TO BUILD ONE OF YOUR **OWN.**

FOR FOUR LONG DAYS ODYSSEUS TOILED.

PUTTING HIS LONG-UNUSED SHIPBUILDING SKILLS TO WORK, HE FASHIONED A ONE-MAN BOAT FOR HIMSELF ...

... AND AT THE END OF THE FOUR DAYS, TOOK THE PROVISIONS CALYPSO HAD GIVEN HIM AND SAILED AWAY ...

...LEAVING A BROKEN-HEARTED GODDESS BEHIND HIM ON THE SAND.

ODYSSEUS SAILED AWAY FROM ALL OF THE PAIN AND HEARTACHE HE HAD ENCOUNTERED ON HIS LONG, LONG JOURNEY ...

... BUT UNKNOWN TO HIM, THERE WAS PLENTY MORE WAITING FOR HIM AT HIS OWN HOME, ON THE ROCKY ISLE OF *ITHACA*.

GLOSSARY AND PRONUNCIATION GUIDE

ATHENA (uh-*thee*-nuh): the Greek goddess of wisdom

CHARYBDIS (kuh-*rib*-duhs): a violent whirlpool that sucks up ships, destroys them, and spits them out

CIRCE (*sur*-see): a witch whom Odysseus and his men encounter on their journey home to Ithaca

CYCLOPS (*sy*-klops): one of a race of mythical giants with a single eye in the middle of their foreheads. The plural form is Cylopes.

DESERT: to flee or abandon one's duties without permission

EURYLOCHUS (yur-*ril*-eh-kus): Odysseus' trusted second-in-command

HELIOS (*hee*-lee-us): the Greek god of the sun

HEPHAISTOS (heh-*fes*-tus): the blacksmith god

HERMES (*hur*-meez): the messenger of the gods on Mount Olympus

ITHACA: Odysseus' homeland; a Greek island

LAISTRYGONIANS (ly-struh-*go*-nee-uns): a race of fierce giants that Odysseus and his men encounter on their journey home to Ithaca

ODYSSEUS (oh-*dis*-see-uhs): king of Ithaca

PENELOPE (peh-*nel*-oh-pee): wife of Odysseus

POLYPHEMUS (pahl-ee-*fee*-muhs): the fearsome Cyclops whom Odysseus and his men encounter on their journey home to Ithaca

POSEIDON (poh-*sy*-duhn): the Greek god of the sea

PROVISIONS: a stock of supplies, such as food and water

SCYLLA (*si*-luh): a six-headed monster that can devour six sailors in one stroke

STRAIT: a narrow passageway connecting two large bodies of water

SUITORS: one who courts a woman or seeks to marry her

TALISMAN: an object that is believed to defend against evil or bring good fortune

TELEMACHUS (tel-*lem*-ah-kus): Odysseus' son

TROJAN WAR: a brutal ten-year war fought between the Trojans and the Greeks around 1200 B.C.

ZEUS (*zoos*): king of the Greek gods

FURTHER READING, WEBSITES, AND MOVIES

Bolton, Lesley. *The Everything Classical Mythology Book: Greek and Roman Gods, Goddesses, Heroes, and Monsters from Ares to Zeus.* Avon, MA: Adams Media Corporation, 2002. This who's who guide introduces young readers to Greek and Roman mythology.

Day, Nancy. *Your Travel Guide to Ancient Greece.* Minneapolis: Twenty-First Century Books, 2001. Day prepares readers for a trip back to ancient Greece, including which cities to visit, how to get around, what to wear, and how to fit in with the locals.

Fontes, Ron, and Justine Fontes. *The Trojan Horse: The Fall of Troy.* Minneapolis: Graphic Universe, 2007. Learn more about the Trojan War, the exciting story that precedes the *Odyssey.*

MythWeb. http://www.mythweb.com/index.html. This site, with a searchable encyclopedia, provides readers with information on gods, goddesses, and places in Greek myth, as well as ample information about Homer's *Odyssey.*

The Odyssey. DVD. Directed by Andrei Konchalovsky. Vancouver, British Columbia, Canada: Lions Gate Entertainment, 1997. This made-for-TV movie stars Armand Assante as Odysseus and uses excellent special effects to portray the thrilling tale of Odysseus' adventures.

CREATING *ODYSSEUS: ESCAPING POSEIDON'S CURSE*

To retell this ancient story for modern readers, Dan Jolley consulted several translations of the *Odyssey,* both prose and verse versions. Artist Thomas Yeates used historical and traditional sources to shape the story's visual details—from images on ancient Greek vases to sculpture and other artwork. David Mulroy of the University of Wisconsin-Milwaukee ensured the accuracy of the story's historical and visual details. Together, the text and the art bring to life this story from ancient Greece.

original pencil from page 28

INDEX

ABOUT THE AUTHOR AND THE ARTIST

DAN JOLLEY began his writing career in the early 1990s. His limited series *Obergeist* was voted Best Horror Comic of 2001 by *Wizard Magazine*, and his DC Comics project *JSA: The Unholy Three* received an Eisner Award nomination (the comics industry's highest honor) for Best Limited Series of 2003. In recent years, he has co-written two novels based on licensed properties: *Star Trek SCE: Some Assembly Required*, and *Vengeance*, from the television series *Angel*. May of 2007 will see the debut of Dan's first solo novel series, an original Young Adult sci-fi espionage story called *Alex, Unlimited*, published by a joint venture of TokyoPop and HarperCollins. Dan lives in Cary, North Carolina, where he spends way too much time playing video games.

THOMAS YEATES began his art training in high school and continued at Utah State University and Sacramento State University. Subsequently, he was a member of the first class at Joe Kubert's School, a trade program for aspiring comic book artists in New Jersey. Yeates has worked as an illustrator for DC Comics, Marvel, Dark Horse, and many other companies, drawing Tarzan, Zorro, the Swamp Thing, Time Spirits, Captain America, and Conan. For the Graphic Myths and Legends series, he illustrated *King Arthur: Excalibur Unsheathed*, *Robin Hood: Outlaw of Sherwood Forest*, and *Atalanta: The Race against Destiny*. Yeates lives in northern California with his wife and daughter.